T0209833

Apples *from* Heaven

Brent Vaughan and Kathy Vaughan

WESTBOW
PRESS®
A DIVISION OF THOMAS NELSON
& ZONDERVAN

WestBow Press books may be ordered through booksellers or by contacting:

WestBow Press
A Division of Thomas Nelson & Zondervan
1663 Liberty Drive
Bloomington, IN 47403
www.westbowpress.com
1 (866) 928-1240

ISBN: 978-1-9736-2723-4 (sc)
ISBN: 978-1-9736-2722-7 (e)

Library of Congress Control Number: 2018905266

Print information available on the last page.

WestBow Press rev. date: 7/2/2018

Contents

Dear Brent,

I've tried several times to write your story, never knowing exactly where to start. It was about a year after you died, while cleaning the home office, that I came across your autobiography. You remember—it's the one you wrote in Mrs. McHugh's class. I'm embarrassed to admit, but I never knew you wrote it. Only after reading it did things became clear as to why you asked me so many questions about our family. I still remember standing at the kitchen sink telling you story after story. It was fun to share those stories with you. I'm so glad that sixth grade was your favorite school year, and I too was disappointed when it ended. You always came home and got everyone excited about the things you were learning, and as a result, Nick and Justin became super-excited about the teachers at school. I am thankful for that. Well, after reading your autobiography, I decided to use it as an outline to help guide my thoughts and finish writing your story. I really miss you, Brent. You were a boy who was truly passionate about living. Your example of someone who trusted God was inspiring to everyone who knew you, especially me. Most remarkably was when you got the devastating news of your failing health at the age of twelve that your enthusiasm continued. I am honored to be able to share your passion, your perspective, and God's incredible power that never stopped shining through you. Being your mom has challenged me to grow in so many crazy ways, and I am grateful to tell the insights I have learned from you. Thanks for letting Jesus's love shine through you always. I'm looking forward to seeing you again and to spending eternity with you in heaven.

Love,
Mom

I

When I Was Born: Congratulations, You Have a Baby Boy

Do not be anxious about anything, but in every situation, by prayer and petition, with thanksgiving, present your requests to God. And the peace of God, which transcends all understanding, will guard your hearts and your minds in Christ Jesus.

—Philippians 4:6–7 NIV

Brent as a baby

1

Hi. My name is Brent Vaughan. I was born on Easter Sunday, March 26, 1989. The doctor noticed something wrong with my heart. On Monday, I was transferred to a downtown-Chicago hospital that specialized in taking care of critically ill children. There, doctors gave my parents the bad news that I had only two weeks to live unless I received a new heart. My heart was missing the left ventricle. My parents put me on a waiting list for a new heart from an organ donor. On Monday, April 3, 1989, I received a new heart through a transplant. After that, my parents and I lived in a small town until June 1991, the year my brother was born. Then we lived with my grandparents until our new house was built. We moved into it in December of 1991. It's been fun living in our house. At our house, we lived so close to Jewel Osco that we called it our pantry. I could also ride my bike to the school, the library, and my grandparents' house. I was very thankful that I could see my grandparents almost any time I want.

It's true; Brent was born on March 26, 1989, at 11:36 a.m. That day just so happened to be Easter Sunday. I had been looking forward to the Easter celebration at our church. I was a bit disappointed when my labor finally started for real the night before, even though I was ten days past due and feeling very uncomfortable. This was the part of becoming a mom that terrified me. Bill and I had taken birthing classes and believed we knew what to expect, but the thought of actually giving birth was not my idea of a good time. To be perfectly honest, I wasn't feeling ready to be a mom either. Bill and I hadn't planned to start our family so soon. Shortly after our wedding, we decided to wait at least five years before we had children. So, after being married for not quite a year, we were shocked to learn that I was pregnant. Looking back, neither one of us felt excited about having a baby; we had so many plans. Our trip to Europe was a dream Bill really wanted to fulfill, and a house in which to raise our children was nowhere in sight. We knew that once kids came along, I would stay at home and become a full-time mom. We thought we would never be able to reach our goals, and selfishly, we both became a little resentful and scared.

The birth was more stressful than Bill and I had imagined. The birthing classes made childbirth seem so beautiful and serene. I'd have to say my experience looked more like an episode of CSI. I was in excruciating pain, and the baby's heart rate dropped suddenly. I refused all pain medication because I was afraid of the side effects on the baby. I resolved to endure the delivery naturally. It didn't sound or look natural, but it was… and the second Brent was born, the pain stopped.

"Congratulations, you have a baby boy!" the medical staff said to me.

I'll never forget seeing him that very first moment. His hands stretched out wide, as if he was grabbing all that life could offer. His perfect little face was combined with what appeared to be a strong, healthy body. He looked huge. Wow! How? What? Where? At birth, he weighed eight pounds, three ounces, and was twenty-two inches long. I was so glad I had decided to deliver him at the hospital. I had debated in my mind over whether to have a home birth, seeing that hospitals were not my favorite places to be. Feeling proud, amazed, and full of this indescribably overwhelming love, we couldn't wait to introduce Brent to everyone we knew. All of a sudden, our dreams, plans, goals, and careers seemed insignificant compared to the privilege of being Brent's parents. Very soon, visitors came to meet the newest member of our family. His full name was Brent William Vaughan. The nurse informed me that they would keep Brent in the nursery during visiting hours to protect him from potential illness and to monitor his heart. A simple heart murmur was detected, but it was nothing to be anxious about, they assured us. Here's a funny thing; I was diagnosed with a heart murmur just months before I got pregnant, so I wasn't worried. My only setback was that I needed to be premedicated every time I saw the dentist. I had no other symptoms. Overall, I had a healthy pregnancy, although my morning sickness lasted the entire time, and I never knew when or where I would get sick. That made life interesting.

The thrill of showing Brent off to our guests eventually ended as our visitors left. Shortly after that, Bill did as well. He needed to get rest and so did I. I tried to sleep, but something in my heart was heavy. I was so excited to be a new mom but couldn't stop wondering if Brent was okay. I kept hearing a baby cry in the nursery down the hall, so I finally asked the nurse to bring him to me. It must have been past midnight, but I didn't mind. I'll never forget holding him. He smelled so sweet. He felt so soft. He looked so different: his skin color appeared dark to me. I questioned the nurse, and she passed it off by saying that his circulation hadn't kicked in yet. She told me there was nothing to be concerned about. I remember holding him tightly and singing "Jesus Loves Me" to him several times. I had this overwhelming need to pray with him and to assure him to not be afraid. If my roommate was still awake, she probably thought I was crazy, but I didn't care. During our time together, I introduced myself to Brent and told him all about his new family members by name. It was amazing to get to know him. The nurse returned a few hours later and encouraged me to send Brent back to the nursery. She suggested that I try to sleep, and again she confidently set my mind at ease. Reluctantly I agreed, and after Brent left, I fell asleep. I am so thankful for the time I spent with him. Those moments will never, ever leave my heart.

Early the next morning, several doctors came in to notify me that Brent was going to be transferred to a better-equipped hospital in downtown Chicago. After a good night's sleep and a shower, Bill returned to the hospital to visit, not realizing what had just happened. Brent was now receiving oxygen in the nursery because he was unable to maintain an adequate level of oxygen breathing on his own; that's why his color had become dark. The transport team arrived with a very specialized incubator, and soon after, they left with Brent. I, too, was discharged so Bill and I could follow. The ride to Chicago seemed endless. The weather outside was unseasonably warm and sunny, yet inside I felt dark and gloomy. I tried to be optimistic. I fought back the tears. We sat quietly for the entire ride to the hospital.

Once we arrived, we waited for what seemed like days. My heart was aching to see and to hold Brent. The guilt was unbearable. If only I had wanted him, this nightmare would not be happening. That was the message I kept playing over and over in my mind. While Brent was being evaluated, Bill and I sat in a small and uncomfortable room. We weren't really talking … just waiting. Every minute that passed felt like a day. Every hour felt like a year. I wanted to hold him so badly. I continued to pray desperately for Brent, all the while hoping that he wasn't scared. How long could an echo take? I figured we'd get the diagnosis and a prescription and be on our way to live out the rest of my perfect story. I sensed, however, that something wasn't right, and over time, I became fearful. We made calls to family and told them the news. Several family members came to support us and thoughtfully provided food, brand-new clothes for me, and many encouraging prayers. While we were waiting, Bill's sister Juni and brother-in-law Brett stopped by and brought us Subway sandwiches. Somehow, that sub was just what I needed to give me the strength to face the team of doctors, nurses, and social workers who came in to give us the news.

Brent was officially diagnosed with hypoplastic left-heart syndrome. He was born with only three chambers in his heart, rather than four. His left ventricle never fully developed during my pregnancy, and that was the reason he was having difficulty breathing on his own. Our treatment options were to bring him home while he lived out his few remaining weeks, to attempt a new procedure that would require many surgeries and an uncertain future, or to seek a new heart, which would have its daily challenges but at the time, seemed to offer us the most hope.

A transplant. I had heard of people having transplants, but I had never personally met anyone who had undergone this procedure. Was it ethical? How did God feel about this procedure, and ultimately, would a heart be available in time? I couldn't imagine leaving Brent at the hospital. Bill and I were both overwhelmed with the responsibility of making this decision, and time was not on our side. Then came the reality-check question: how could we pray for our son to receive a new heart? We couldn't! To pray for someone else to walk the path we feared was unthinkable. All we could do was to pray for God to give us the strength to walk through whatever door He opened. We knew that either outcome was going to be difficult. For Brent to die would be unbearable. For Brent to live would be overwhelming. I wasn't sure we could take on the responsibility of his care or the financial burden. We were told that his needs were going to be great.

The moment we both had been waiting for finally came. We got to see Brent. He looked peaceful, and his perfect little face contradicted the machines and the monitors that were intimidating. I was exhausted, both physically and emotionally. It's in moments like these when you realize how quickly life can change. I wanted so desperately to take Brent home and to wake up from this horrible nightmare. I wish I could have stood there longer, but by then Bill and I were both exhausted and my body would not let me. We decided to leave, knowing we had a decision to make and we didn't have much time. The doctors made themselves available for us throughout the night. Any questions we had, they would try to answer. My parents opened their home for us to unwind and provided us with a nice meal. We had to choose if we were going to take Brent home, attempt the surgery, or put him on the list for a new heart by the next day.

It was now Tuesday morning, and we were on our way back to the hospital. I remembered being in labor and wishing it was Wednesday. At the time I figured that by then, all the pain would be over and the three of us would be home beginning our new life together. Well it was only Tuesday, and all I wanted to do was to scream, *"Time out."* This was not the story I signed up for. If someone asked me if I wanted to change God's plan for my life I would have said *yes*! I imagined being able to rewind the tape and edit this scene. Slowly I was learning that life is not about my plans; it's about living out God's plan for His glory and eventually having a story to share. The questions started coming, not only in my heart, but also through the voices of those around me: How did this happen? Was it something I did while I was pregnant? Was it because we didn't plan to start our family yet? Despite all the questions for which we were hoping for answers, the doctors were unable to give us a reason as to why Brent's heart did not develop properly. They called it a fluke of nature. Trying to understand and needing an explanation became insignificant compared to the decision we needed to make. Completely shutting myself out from the world around me, I found comfort in God's word. I was strengthened and encouraged by Philippians 4:6–7, "Do not be anxious about anything, but in every situation, by prayer and petition, with thanksgiving, present your requests to God. And the peace of God, which transcends all understanding, will guard your hearts and your minds in Christ Jesus." Rehearsing those verses over and over in my mind allowed me to live in His peace. On my own I felt numb, scared, inadequate, overwhelmed, and guilty. With God's truth and strength, I felt confident, secure, and above all honored that He chose me to be Brent's mom. Trusting that God would provide what we needed and the courage to do our part, Brent was put on the list for a new heart.

Our wait would not be long, and Bill and I continued to commute to the city daily. A friend or family member would pick me up at home and drive me to my Mom's house so I could wait for Bill to finish work. Thankfully, he was only working half days during that time. That gave us most of the day/evening to be with Brent. I was unable to drive, per doctor rules, and I could barely sit anyway. I eventually found out that I broke my tail bone during the delivery. Just like our first ride downtown, neither one of us ever talked much on our way to the hospital; I think we were afraid of what we would face once we got there. Bill carried a pager provided by the transplant team so that if/when the doctors needed to get a hold of us, they could. Each visit, our time with Brent was amazing. Even though he was too weak to open his eyes, his presence somehow gave us hope and strength. We would stand by his crib for hours and bring cards or letters made by family and friends. I would gently hold his hand or caress his head while we talked to him and read the cards and letters. We even bought little books and toys to keep close by. We tape recorded encouraging words for him so the nurses could play it for Brent while we weren't there. I didn't want him to feel alone. As encouraging as our daily visits were, it was also difficult as I wanted to hold him so badly. But for some reason, it was never presented as an option, and at the time I never considered asking. As time went on, Brent continued to hold his own, yet each day we could see him grow weaker. I wondered if he understood what we were saying, and I wondered if he knew how much everyone loved him. I wondered if he was scared, and I desperately hoped that eventually he would come home.

April 1 was an extremely difficult day for me. I was so exhausted from the week before. Not really being able to sleep, eat, or even think for that matter, I literally collapsed on our way out the door to visit Brent. I did not want to be alone, and thankfully, Bill agreed to stay at home with me. We called the hospital several times throughout the day to check on Brent. The nurses were amazing. They assured us that they would talk to Brent and that if anything changed, they would call us immediately. That day felt like the longest day of my life. Still not being able to sleep, I was somehow able to regain enough strength to visit the next day. It was Sunday, and on our way to the hospital, things were quiet as usual, and the ride seemed to take forever. Instead of racing up to the eighth floor like we usually did, I stopped to take a quick bathroom break near the main entrance. The next thing I remember happening was that Bill rushed into the women's bathroom, telling me, "I got paged, I got paged." This could mean only one of two things; Brent's health was declining rapidly, or a new heart was found. We both felt confident that our prayers had been answered and we raced upstairs. Shocked at how quickly we responded to the page, the nurses confirmed that indeed a new heart was found and that Brent would be heading to surgery very soon. We did not leave his bedside; we couldn't. We were excited, scared, and also feeling extremely sorrowful; the thing we feared the most was now a reality for another family. The impact of their decision to give Brent a second chance was overpowering. How could we ever truly thank them? Gratefully, we had several hours to wait before the time came. It was late into the night when the transplant team came to take Brent to the operating room. They allowed us to walk with him, we said our good-byes, and I cautiously watched while holding my breath as the operating doors closed.

On April 3, 1989, God opened the door for Brent to have a second chance at life. As strange as this may sound, during his surgery, I made myself fall asleep, and Bill did the same. Several people came to be with us, but I needed to shut down. I did not want to talk to anyone or listen to anyone talk to me. Being strong at this time was not an option. When I was awake, all I could think about was what was happening in the surgery room. Every so often the head nurse would come out and give us an update. She would have to wake us up, and I know she probably began to wonder what kind of parents we would be. The surgery was finally over, and the nurse told us to be prepared to talk to the surgeons. I felt so sick that my stomach was in knots. I needed something to eat, and Bill needed fresh air. He decided to get donuts at the shop down the street. A little fresh air would do him some good, and since I hadn't eaten anything at all the day before or throughout the night, a little something was appealing. We both wanted to be alert and ready to hear what the doctors had to say. The lead surgeon came out sooner than expected and was *enraged* when I told him that Bill was out getting donuts. He boldly asked if we fully understood what had just happened and if we realized the full impact and responsibility of taking care of a baby like Brent. I was taken back to say the least but understood his frustration. It did look bad … but within seconds of this encounter, Bill returned. He must have run to get the donuts because he was only gone a few minutes. We were briefed on Brent's surgery, and as far as they could tell, all went well. The next forty-eight hours would be critical. Rejection and infection were our new enemies.

We asked if we could see Brent and they agreed, but they strongly cautioned us to not be discouraged by what we saw. Nothing could have prepared me. At first I was excited to see him, thinking that I would be optimistic and hopeful. Since there was a new protocol in place, it took some time for us to dress to enter his room. As we were wearing the sterile outfits, the only parts visible to Brent were our eyes. I was completely covered when I entered the room, and I was surprised at the sense of regret and fear I felt. The bandage on his chest was almost as big as he was. He was now on a ventilator and had several more IVs pumping into him, along with several more monitors. Our visit was brief, and we both wanted to stay longer, but since Brent was still asleep, we were encouraged to go home and get some rest, so we agreed to leave. Things were stable, and if any changes took place, the medical team assured us they would contact us immediately. We lived about two hours away from the hospital and had been home for a short time when suddenly the pager went off; we were called back. Brent's new heart had stopped beating normally, and the doctors were very concerned. Bill and I hurried back to the hospital. It took the team of doctors several hours to figure out what had happened; the central line in his neck clotted, and all the pumps continued to infuse fluid into his body. The adrenaline had kicked in, and horror filled my heart when we walked into Brent's room. He was now wide awake, and his eyes were open. Streams of tears were pouring from his swollen face. We couldn't hear a thing due the ventilator, but you could tell he was screaming. His eyes did all the talking, and this is what they were saying to me: "Why did you let them do this to me?" I kept apologizing and struggled to see him like that. We stood at his bedside, and I quietly began to plead with the Lord to take him home, but not home with me. I begged Him to take Brent to heaven. I knew that if he went to heaven, he would no longer have to suffer like this. In such a short amount of time, Bill and I were flooded with a wide range of emotion. From ecstatic highs to frightening lows, we clung to the prayers of so many family and friends, which literally carried us through. Later that same day we learned that while the central line was clotting, Brent's heart miraculously began to slow down. That saved his life. With so many people praying, I believe the Lord caused his new heart to deliberately become weak. The side effects were not easy to witness; he was so puffy from the IVs that his perfect little face looked strange. He had additional chest tubes inserted to remove the extra fluid. Being completely gowned to protect him from infection, all Brent could see was our eyes; I was hoping he would know that it was me.

Gently stroking his head and gently touching his face, I was disturbed to notice that when I pressed on his cheek, it took hours for my fingerprint to go away; that's how bloated he was. The doctors were frustrated that this had happened, and they were uncertain if this setback would cause any lasting effects.

As the days continued, I remember the trouble we had getting him off the ventilator. It was a fight all its own. While intubated, Brent struggled to recover and was unable to eat by mouth. Once the ventilator was removed, he still had difficulty eating by mouth, so he was being fed by an NG tube. He began projectile vomiting as the formula was unable to pass through to his stomach. The doctors were determined to treat him for what they thought was rejection while the whole time he had another undetected birth defect. The head nurse who was taking care of Brent in the ICU continued to insist that Brent had all the classic symptoms of pyloric stenosis. I am so glad she did not give up her fight. After several days and doses of strong medication, Brent was still not responding to the anti-rejection treatment; his vomiting continued and even got worse. The doctors finally agreed to do a simple upper GI to rule out the stenosis. I was in his room when the GI team came to take Brent for his procedure. I walked with the team of specialists down the hall and stayed in the room with Brent and watched the entire procedure. Once again, the medical team was amazing. They treated Brent with such care and grace, just like I would have if I were doing the procedure myself. They talked gently to him and even reassured him the entire time. He didn't seem bothered by the test at all. Although once it was confirmed that he had pyloric stenosis, Brent's primary cardiologist told me that Brent was going to be scheduled for another surgery immediately. *What*! Another surgery? *Wait* … He just got off the ventilator. It took Brent so long to get off it we were concerned about him having another surgery. What would this do to his heart? How would this affect his chance at getting off the ventilator again? We were reassured that this surgery would be 100 percent effective and relatively simple to perform. We were also encouraged to learn that since Brent was now able to breathe on his own, his chance of getting off the ventilator the second time was expected to be easier. Thankfully he recovered from his second surgery, just as expected.

With each day that passed, Brent grew stronger and became more alert.

During the last week of his hospitalization, I was able to stay overnight in his room with him so I could learn to be his primary caregiver at home, and Bill came to visit every evening. On the weekend Bill stayed overnight with us as well. The nursing staff and the doctors were extremely supportive and encouraging. They taught us how to take Brent's vitals and helped us to understand all his medications. Together we learned to watch for signs of rejection and infection, and all the while I was building my confidence to be Brent's mom, and Bill was determined to be the best dad.

2 My Early Years: Hi Dad

My son, if your heart is wise, then my heart will be glad indeed.

—Proverbs 23:15 NIV

Brent and Bill sitting on the beach

When my parents brought me home from the hospital for the first night, my parents and I were all in bed when all of the sudden I said, "Hi, Dad." I was only five weeks old. My mom and dad both laughed. My parents would always read to me. When I was little, I would never eat. One time my mom made me seven different meals for dinner and even tried feeding me in the bathtub.

～

May 3, 1989, still is at the top of the list for my most *amazing* day. I'll never forget our first night home. I was more than ready to leave the hospital, but I remember Bill felt a little anxious. Brent's nursery had been patiently waiting for him this whole time, and when we finally walked into our home, it felt fabulous to be there. We were a family! It took some time until we got organized, and eventually we put Brent in his crib for the night. Neither one of us wanted to put him down. He was so happy, and so were we. Bill and I finally got settled in our own bed, and we seriously heard Brent say, "Hi, Dad." It was so clear. We laughed ourselves silly. In reality Brent should have said, "Thanks, Dad!" Bill was no longer focused on his needs, dreams, or aspirations. He gladly accepted his role as provider and took advantage of every opportunity to work. To this day he is by far the hardest-working man I know!

We did everything we could to keep Brent healthy and happy. In reality, we couldn't have survived all the stress of everyday life without the love and support of our families. Things weren't always perfect, but there was never a doubt in our minds about the fact that we were loved and cared for. My sister Pam was a nurse and took it upon herself to help me find the right stethoscope and blood pressure cuff for use at home. She also offered to babysit for Brent when he first came home from the hospital, which was such a blessing. My brother-in-law, Glenn, and my dad made repairs to our house to make it safe for Brent, while my sister, Liz, would stop in to clean our home anytime Brent was in the hospital. My mom brought groceries and cooked meals and helped by driving us to Brent's clinic appointments to allow Bill time for work. Tami and Tom gave Bill flexible work hours and provided lots of opportunity for overtime. Tami and Juni babysat when they could and would send sweet cards of encouragement in the mail. Bill's brother, Keek, and Keek's wife, Kim, came over often and made life really fun. Eventually, I created a babysitting schedule where several family and friends took turns sitting for us so Bill and I could work on our relationship. Every Wednesday I looked forward to getting out, and even though our dates weren't fancy, they were extremely important to help us build a strong marriage.

Although we were considered outpatient, we still spent quite a bit of time at the hospital. For the first three months of Brent's life at home; we were going to clinic twice a week. It was reassuring to have lab results and the transplant team to evaluate him to rule out any sign of rejection or infection. I continued to grow confident as Brent's mom as well. Watching him endure blood draws *never* got easy for me. Overall, teaching Brent about Jesus was my number-one priority. I read the Bible and other books to him constantly. I prayed over him and taught him to worship. I was so thankful for the gift of a second chance that God provided and for all the people who partnered with us. Being admitted back into the hospital was not an option in my opinion, yet it did happen. Brent struggled with ear infections, and that would cause him to become violently ill. He needed IV fluids, and at times IV medications to prevent him from further complications. My days were filled with his care, and Bill's were filled with work. We were both so busy that we didn't even have time to realize that some of our friends had backed away. The love I felt for Brent was the most amazing thing I could ever imagine. He developed and grew the way he should, although getting him to gain weight was nearly impossible. Despite his terrible eating habits, he amazed us constantly. His love for life was contagious, even as an infant. Even when he couldn't speak, his eyes did all the talking. When we were told we could start coming to clinic one time a week, I was excited and a bit nervous. Yes, it was a challenge to get to clinic, yet the reassurance was something I felt I needed. Over the months and years, we eventually weaned down to every other week, one time a month, and finally we were only going downtown for emergency visits and for his annual study.

Not only were we learning how to evaluate and interpret Brent's personality, but we also focused on his blood counts, oxygen levels, heart rates, blood pressure readings, and medication levels. I was also forced to understand EOBs, deductibles, claims, out-of-pocket expenses, copays, and collections. It took some time for me to figure out what all that paperwork meant. I spent countless hours matching EOBs with what seemed like millions of bills that were consistently flowing in. I was fortunate to have amazing help from an unexpected source. Her name was Julie. Julie worked for the insurance company and took it upon herself to become Brent's advocate and my friend. Whenever I had a question about a claim, I knew Julie would find the answer. Every time I called, she would say, "Before we talk business, how's my baby doing?" I would give her all the updates, and as I was talking, I could hear her smile! Julie was such a blessing to me. She never made me feel stupid and patiently explained the answers to all my questions. I remember the day we got a $10,000 bill from the hospital for Brent's first surgery. Mind you, the bill was over seven years old. The notice stated that the bill was past due, and if not paid within ten days, we would be sent to collections. Somehow the hospital forgot to charge us for the procurement and decided to bill us several years after the fact. I was super frustrated! After I gave Julie the update on Brent's health and activities, she calmly replied, "Don't worry, honey. Consider it paid in full." I never got another notice for that bill. It was paid in full.

The Lord also had an incredible way of showing up, through unexpected gifts, caring strangers, and our amazing, supportive families. In particular I remember getting ready to celebrate Brent's second Christmas. Just weeks before the holiday, we got an unexpected hospital bill in the mail that equaled all of the money we had set aside for presents. Not wanting to fall behind in paying the hospital, Bill and I decided to forego all gifts that year, and we were blown away just days after the payment was made. A simple card was delivered to our home signed by our pastor, and it read, "Someone thought you could use this." The amount we received matched the exact amount I had paid. We celebrated Christmas with a new perspective—confidence in the fact that the Lord will keep His promises even without us asking. We never told anyone that we were in need of money, nor did we ask the Lord to provide extra for Christmas. He just did.

Caring strangers still remind me to be grateful. Several people were aware of our circumstances, yet many had no idea of the strain the medical bills had on us. One Sunday after church, Steve G. approached my parents, asking how things were going. My parents were excited to tell Steve that Brent was doing well and that he was now a big brother. As grandparents do, I'm sure they were in full brag mode. Steve continued to question and specifically asked about how we were getting along financially. He was interested in helping us as he knew of a fund that was available to help families in our situation. My parents introduced us, and over time Steve gladly handed several bills to the bank that held the funds collected by generous community members for a family whose son was in need of a liver transplant. Sadly, the young boy passed away before his surgery, leaving behind the money. Steve's caring heart connected our paths and made our lives a bit easier.

3

My Family: Control Yourself; You're the Grown-up!

Every good and perfect gift is from above, coming down from the Father of the heavenly lights, who does not change like shifting shadows.

—James 1:17

A family portrait outdoors

My dad's name is William Blue Vaughan III. He is an air pollution-control specialist. He loves to travel all around, which he usually does because of his job. My mom's name is Katharina Marie Vaughan. She graduated from Northern Illinois University with a bachelor's of science degree in art education. She's a full-time mom. She loves to garden, cook, and be a mom. I have three awesome brothers and a little sister. I am the oldest of the five of us. Nick, Justin, and Kevin are all interested in archaeology because at home I'm always talking about it. Corrina told us that when she grows up, she wants to be an eye doctor and a mommy.

⁓

I love how Brent described our family. Looking back, I remember him asking me so many questions, but I'm sad to say I didn't really pay attention as to why. Brent was an excellent student. He never needed reminding to study or to complete his work. He loved school, mostly because he got to be with his friends. Finding his autobiography was such an indescribable gift.

⁓

Nick, the second oldest, is really funny. He's really mature for a fourth grader.

⁓

Nick was born November 13, 1990. Once again, we were surprised to be pregnant. It was strongly suggested to us that we not have any more children due to the nature of Brent's birth defect. Even though we didn't plan it, I did my best to enjoy this pregnancy and waited with great anticipation to meet this new little person. Overall my pregnancy with Nick went well. Nothing was out of the ordinary for me, and our level II ultrasound showed that we were having a boy who had all four chambers of his heart. We were excited to add Nicholas to our family. Brent was super excited to be a *big brother*. He was so intrigued by Nick. He would often just sit and watch him. Brent would help in any way he could. He loved Nick, and Nick loved Brent. Only twenty months apart, they were best friends from the start. At first Brent called Nick, "Licky." I'm not sure if he did that just to get a laugh, but there was never a time Brent acted or seemed jealous. In the beginning Nick would follow Brent around the room with his eyes, and eventually as he grew, Nick would shadow him on foot. Brent was a bit cautious, and Nick was extremely adventurous. He climbed, jumped, and flipped on just about everything. Soon he realized he could take Brent down. Brent would never fight back or stand up for himself, so I finally had to encourage him to step up and not allow Nick to pick on him. In time Brent learned to stand up for himself and fell nicely into the role of leader. Adding Nick to our family not only gave Brent a playmate, but he also helped make us a more normal family. In my heart I would often compare Nick to a cold, refreshing cup of water on a very hot day. Life could not have been better. God's blessings were amazing!

Nick was more than just Brent's little brother. He had and still has great insight. Whenever Brent was away, Nick would take the role of leader. At the age of five, knowing that I was terrified of mice, Nick decided to play it cool the day a mouse decided to visit our house. Brent was at school, and the other three boys were home with me. I was busy doing laundry, and that's when Nick thought it was time to let me in on a little secret he had discovered.

He quietly came up to me, cupped his hands over my ear, and whispered to me, "Mom, I saw something in the TV room, but it wasn't a mouse."

Panicked, I immediately called Bill at work and begged him to come home because Nick told me he saw something that might be a mouse. Bill was annoyed because he was busy and told me to call him if I saw that "something" for real. I was so *mad* that I decided to take matters into my own hands. I marched into the TV room and noticed a brown blanked draped over the arm of the couch. I suspected that the blanket had somehow moved and that's what Nick saw. I quickly picked up the blanket and looked all around … nothing. *Phew.* Not long after that, the boys and I were eating lunch. Nick, Justin, and I were sitting at the kitchen table, and Kevin was minding his own business seated next to me in his high chair.

I can't remember what we were eating, but I do remember that Nick got all pale faced and very calmly said, "Ah, Mom, that thing I told you that I saw … well … it's right there," as he was pointing down the hall.

Being completely out of control and out of my mind, I began to scream hysterically. I jumped up on the counter, and the boys immediately hopped onto their chairs as the mouse ran into the empty living room. With nowhere to hide, it raced into the kitchen and hid under the stove, and I continued to scream. All three boys were terrified. Frozen in fear, they too stood on their chairs, except Kevin because he was strapped in his highchair. However, we were all screaming and crying. Immediately I called Bill again, and he told me that he would come home as soon as he could.

After I screamed for longer than I should have, Nick finally yelled as loud as he could over my irrational voice, *"Hey, control yourself. You're the grown-up. You're scaring me."*

Well, that shocked me, but it didn't stop me. I still acted irrationally. Bill came home to find all of us crying, screaming, and standing on the kitchen chairs. The poor, tiny mouse had a nervous breakdown while it cowered under the stove. Bill handled the situation graciously. He gathered the boys and held Kevin tightly in his arms and collected the tiny field mouse into a bin and had the boys help him release it into the wild. I'm not sure Kevin or the mouse ever really recovered from that. I'm glad Kevin doesn't remember.

—⁓—

Justin, who is third oldest, is only in second grade but is really smart. I guess he gets it from me. He's the easiest to pick on, so he is usually the victim for a treatment of teasing.

—⁓—

Seeing the bond between Brent and Nick, Bill and I began to think about having another child. Brent was doing well and our in-patient trips to the hospital were becoming less and less, yet the potential of something happening to Brent was still a reality. Together, without the consent of our doctors, we decided to try to have another baby. To say we were excited to be expecting is an understatement. This pregnancy did not come easy. During my level II ultrasound, we discovered that Justin had a cyst on his brain. *Ugh.* The prenatal specialist strongly encouraged us to terminate our baby. Bill and I knew that was not an option for us, and we immediately named Justin that day and began to pray that God would heal him.

Justin arrived June 30, 1993, perfectly healthy. It was amazing to have three beautiful boys. Brent and Nick were definitely excited about their new baby brother, but they were openly disappointed that all he did was sleep and eat. They tag teamed with each other and added Justin to their club once he was old enough to play with them. Justin made me feel like mother of the year. He was the happiest and most content baby I've ever met. His giggle was contagious, and he loved taking naps. On days that I took Brent and Nick to activities, I would drop Justin off at my mom's. As soon as we pulled into her driveway, he would say, "ni-night," and he'd excitedly settle down in his crib with his favorite pillow.

Sending Brent off to school worried me. The risk of infection from being immune-suppressed threatened our world. Putting Brent in a classroom with other children made me feel very unsure. Gladly, I wasn't alone and found courage and support from another family we met while at the hospital in downtown Chicago. Their son was born weeks after Brent with the same heart defect, and he also had a transplant as an infant. He was heading off to kindergarten as well. Together we investigated our options and encouraged each other every step of the way. To hold our boys back from living a "normal" life would not be fair. Amazingly, school became a place where Brent would shine. All the stress of anxiously waiting and seeing that day approach made it seem normal for me to have skipped my cycle. Then came the morning sickness, and before Bill and I could get used to the idea of adding another member to our family, I lost the baby. That hit hard. Heaven was now on the forefront of my mind. After a roller coaster of emotions and the business of life, we pressed on to be the best parents we could.

〜

Kevin, who's second to last, is really energetic. He's always fun to play with. He's going to kindergarten next year.

〜

Kevin's birth was such a celebration. We decided to try to have another baby nine months after the miscarriage. While I was pregnant with Kevin, I had my own health challenges. I was secretly hoping for a girl, yet

Bill and I were excited that we were having another boy and desperately wanted a good outcome. As Kevin grew, I remember being so amazed at his intelligence. Before he could walk, he desperately wanted to be a big boy like his brothers. One of my favorite memories of Kevin was when he was nine months old. We set up a basketball court in the basement with two Little Tikes basketball hoops on either end. The boys were really into the Chicago Bulls, and they played basketball every day. We'd blast the Chicago Bulls CD on the boom box, and the boys would wear their favorite team jerseys. On special days I'd "color" their hair so they could all have turns being Dennis Rodman. Kevin always wanted to join in, and being the great brothers they were, they let him have turns too! Kevin crawled around the floor while the other three were jumping, running, and slam dunking in all directions. It was pure craziness. Once Kevin got the ball, he'd "throw" it, and it would roll. He was having so much fun he would crawl to get it and "throw" it again. Well one time he threw the ball but couldn't find it. He sat up, looked all around, and said, "Where did my basketball go?" Those were Kevin's first words—not mama or dada; he said an entire sentence! *We all laughed hysterically.* It wasn't long after that we realized he knew his numbers and was beginning to recognize the letters of the alphabet.

～

Finally, last but not least, there's Corrina. She is three years old, and she is extremely smart for her age.

～

With four energetic boys, Bill and I decided that our family was complete. I sobbed at the kitchen sink only weeks after Kevin was born. I was ashamed but unable to stop crying, and Bill started to get worried that I had done something terrible. I finally admitted that I was super disappointed that we would never have a little girl. To my delight and surprise, he grabbed me and hugged me and told me that he thought about that as well.

He said, "Maybe someday we will have a granddaughter."

That was enough for me. The idea of having a girl in the family was still a possibility, yet I didn't realize how soon she would come. Kevin was only a little over a year when morning sickness reared its ugly head once more. There was no disguising it. I knew I was pregnant. *How in the world did this happen?* We had just given all our baby things away.

For some reason, deep in my heart I knew that something was wrong with this baby. My ultrasound confirmed my fears. The little girl growing inside me had multiple cysts on both sides of her brain. Once again the prenatal specialist strongly encouraged us to terminate our pregnancy. This time I so wanted to be angry … mostly at God. Why would He allow this? Instead, I decided to be thankful and bought a journal to remind myself of all the blessings in my life. Each day before I got out of bed, I wrote one thing I was thankful for, even if it was just my pillow. This time I prayed for God to give me the strength to deal with whatever the outcome was. I also asked Him to give me the ability to love this new little girl. Somehow I managed to get through the pregnancy. Not only was this emotionally difficult, but it was also physically challenging. I was sick the entire time. Most days I would make it to the kitchen, only to find myself lying on the kitchen floor … the cold floor temporarily stopped my head from spinning long enough so I wouldn't pass out and gave me the strength to call my mom. She would come over and finish getting the boys ready for school. At the time Bill worked close by and was able to come home for lunch. He took care of that meal as I made myself comfortable on the couch. Poor Kevin was frustrated because he didn't understand why I couldn't hold him or play with him.

The three older boys were extremely excited to be adding another baby into our family. Brent would often ask, "When are you going to have another baby?" A sister was even more exciting to them; well not all of them. Kevin was very upset. Looking back on things now, I realize that he just needed me to be his mommy and not the crabby fat lady on the couch. He wanted so desperately to fit in with the older boys too! Justin was now in kindergarten, and that left Kevin at home alone with me. Not only was I sick; I was *huge*. It didn't take long for my belly to hit my thighs when I walked. Bill was afraid we were having triplets or at least twins. Corrina was born nine days late on Good Friday, and we celebrated Easter Sunday at home as a family. Still concerned that her brain was not properly developed, I was reassured by Corrina herself. As I was sitting in my rocking chair all alone in my room while holding her close, she smiled at me. It was a real smile. After having four kids, I knew a smile when I saw one. Our eyes connected, and when they did she said, "I'm okay, Mom. I really am!" My heart felt a peace that reassured me, and since then I've never doubted that she was all right.

As Corrina's strong personality and curiosity developed, Brent would often say, "Now I know why people beat their children." Let me explain: Corrina was always ten steps ahead of me. You'd think that cabinet locks would be mandatory for a house filled with boys. Not the case. It wasn't until Corrina turned two that I finally decided to take a quick trip to the store. It was a Sunday evening, and all the kids were asleep. Earlier that week we bought a brand-new kitchen table, and earlier that day Corrina got into the art cabinet and used a permanent marker to decorate it. I was frustrated because I never knew what she would get into. Bill put the locks on all the cabinets that night after the kids were in bed, and you can't even begin to imagine the *shock* I felt when I came down stairs the next morning. Corrina was standing with her hands on her hips, with all the cabinet doors wide open and saying, "I don't know why Daddy put these things on the cabinets; it just makes them harder to open." The locks stayed on the doors for years just to remind us that Corrina was in charge.

At the age of three she was tired of waiting. I distinctly remember that day as we were going to the library. I asked the boys to get their shoes on while I ran downstairs to start another load of laundry. In the meantime, Corrina took it upon herself to start the car while it was in the garage with the garage door down, because apparently I wasn't coming fast enough. Thankfully Justin quickly informed me, and I realized that leaving the keys in the car was no longer a smart idea. This girl was wearing me out. Not long after that, Corrina decided that she was determined to learn how to ride a two-wheeled bike without training wheels. She politely asked me if I would help her remove the training wheels. Knowing how much effort it took Bill to run around the block with each of the boys, I quickly decided to save that job for him. I told her to wait for Daddy to come home. Without anyone's help, she decided to take matters into her own hands. I decided to go looking for her since things were unusually quiet. When I stepped out into the garage, all I could see was the wrench, training wheels, and hardware on the garage floor scattered about. She was up the street riding her bike all by herself. No one ever had to run around the block with her.

4 Early School Days: I Knew You'd Come

No one will be able to stand against you all the days of your life. As I was with Moses, so I will be with you; I will never leave you nor forsake you.

—Joshua 1:5

Brent standing in front of the kindergarten center sign

In kindergarten I attended the high school. In kindergarten, one of the only friends I still remember is Billy. We had a Hawaiian unit, and we pretended to go on a plane to Hawaii.

———

I'm embarrassed to admit this, but I actually forgot to pick Brent up from school on his very first day of kindergarten. Oh, I was so worried about sending him that walking him to school that day seemed surreal. He was so excited and confident. I held back the tears and watched with a happy heart as he waited in line to enter the building with his new classmates. Once I got home, I kept myself super busy to keep from thinking about how much I missed him, and of course I didn't even want to think about the germs. Before I knew it, I was very late and felt super embarrassed when I got to the school to pick him up. Brent was sitting on the front steps waiting with his teacher. Of course I apologized and was worried that Brent would be upset.

He stood up, smiled, and said, "I'm not mad. I knew you'd come."

After Brent was in school for some time while still in kindergarten, he announced that he was surprised that he was the only kid in his class who had a heart transplant. We never kept that fact a secret. He heard the word *transplant* and knew that his heart was sick when he was a baby, but until this moment he didn't think it was anything that unusual. As I was tucking him in for bed that same night, the question that I knew that would eventually come came ... but I wasn't prepared to answer.

"Where did they get my new heart?" he asked.

Trying not to look surprised or troubled, I quickly prayed and asked the Lord to give me the right words.

"Well, Brent, they got it from another hospital," I said confidently. I was getting ready to leave his room and end the conversation, and I was stunned by what he said next.

"Oh, I see ... someone died and they put the heart into a jar and then gave it to me."

Relieved that his mind was able to put that together without me having to explain made me smile and burst out into laughter. I hugged him so tight. I asked him how he felt about that and explained that his life was a miracle. He seemed okay with the whole transplant thing and eventually got excited about sharing his story with others.

I also remember helping in his classroom. I couldn't help but notice how adorable some of the girls were in his class. I specifically remember this one girl in particular who had very lovely, long blond hair. I don't remember her name, but I asked Brent about her when he got home after my visit.

I asked him if he thought she was cute, and to my surprise, this is what he said: "Ah, there's no hope. I've seen her mother." He paused and then continued. "I don't understand how such a pretty girl can grow up to be such a weathered woman." Interesting that he would put that together at such a young age, because once I saw this little girl's mom, I understood what he meant. She was obviously a heavy drinker and smoker.

—

In first grade I attended Robert Crown School … In first grade my class had a crayfish as a class pet. In indoor recess I would always play checkers with my other classmates.

—

When Brent was in first grade, he wanted his transplant to remain anonymous to his peers. Bringing his juice to school and taking his medicine was embarrassing to him. No one else had to do that, and he didn't want to be different. I respected his desire to be private and let Brent find his way. He enjoyed his time away from home and began making new friends.

5 My School Life: Boiling Eggs

The fear of the LORD is the beginning of knowledge, but fools despise wisdom and instruction.

—Proverbs 1:7

Brent on his bike wearing a red and white jacket

In second through sixth grade, I was able to ride my bike to school because we lived so close … In second grade I was an awesome speller. I would always get one or two wrong, if not one hundred percent. Mario and Ashley were in my class in second grade too.

———

Keeping busy and distracted was easy while Brent was at school. First, Nick, Justin, Kevin, and eventually Corrina needed care, and second, my weekly chores kept me occupied. Typically I was doing seven loads of laundry a day, not to mention meals, dusting/vacuuming, shopping, and dishes. I'll never forget the day I was boiling eggs. Well, actually I did forget at the time. I placed a pan of water on the stove with six eggs to boil. Something caught my attention upstairs, and over an hour later, I was reminded about the eggs when I heard an obnoxious blast. I ran to the kitchen to find that all the water had been cooked out of the pan and the overcooked eggs had exploded *everywhere*. The ceiling, cabinets, floor, and even carpet in the dining room were generously covered with egg. The smell was awful, and it lasted longer than anyone wanted.

When second grade came, Brent decided on his own that it was time to tell the class about his transplant. He wanted to wait a few weeks into the school year to give his classmates enough time to get to know him as Brent, not the transplant boy. He decided that October would be just the right time. I contacted the hospital downtown and asked the transplant nurse if she could come to Brent's school to explain to his class about his remarkable journey. He was both nervous and excited. In the early morning on the day the nurse was scheduled to speak, she called to let us know that there had been an emergency at the hospital the night before and she needed to reschedule. Brent was so disappointed. Somehow I was asked to step in and present Brent's story to his class myself. I felt honored that he would allow me to do that. I quickly put together a few pictures of Brent before and after his transplant. I also brought in his stethoscope, blood pressure cuff, and oral syringe. When I finished the talk, all the kids clapped, and Brent ran up to me and gave me a *huge* hug. I continued to visit his classroom each October until he reached the sixth grade. By then, he was comfortable enough to share his story on his own. Overall Brent continued to do well; he grew physically, socially, and spiritually. He always had us laughing. He was a very clever boy.

~

In third grade my teacher would always read to us. She loved M&Ms.

~

Mrs. Tait was Brent's third-grade teacher. At the time Bill and I felt a bit worried. She loved Brent and just thought he was the funniest kid in town. I'll never forget our parent-teacher conference. Bill and I sat down at the round table in the front of the room with her. Immediately she started to laugh hysterically. She couldn't stop. She finally composed herself long enough to let us know how much fun it was to have Brent in her class. His clever wit was above the rest of the students, and it was appreciated. Mrs. Tait and Brent had tons of fun that year. Looking back now, I am so thankful. He needed that more than anything …

~

In fourth grade my teacher loved Cheetos and pop. One of my most favorite field trips was in fourth grade. We went to the Shed Aquarium in Chicago. We also had a rainforest unit in fourth grade. For an assignment everyone had to pick an animal to do a report on. I had to do the giant armadillo. It was fun.

~

Fourth grade wasn't Brent's favorite year, mostly because his teacher did not appreciate his wit—at first, that is. Watching Brent grow up, I quickly realized that he used humor to deal with the stress of his everyday life. Most days things went smoothly, but I also began to notice that at times he felt different from those around him, and that bothered him. Overall he was genuinely happy, and his enthusiasm was something I realized needed to be protected. Together, Brent's teacher and I decided to meet monthly to discuss his behavior. She did not like his comments or interruptions that were once encouraged. It was very important to me that we carefully broke

Brent's will but not his spirit. Eventually he got the checks off his progress report for talking out of turn, and through our meetings Mrs. Kirchoff and I became good friends.

Brent had dreams for his future and often made goals to achieve them on his own. His love for Egypt brought us to the Field Museum several times, and we never missed a show, movie, or event that had to do with King Tut or pyramids. He also used part of his paper route money to subscribe to *Biblical Archeology* magazine and began his own collection of Egyptian artifacts. When he was still in fourth grade, he came home from school absolutely disgusted. He couldn't believe that his teacher did not know who Howard Carter was. Feeling embarrassed, I quietly admitted that I didn't know who he was either, and Brent proudly proclaimed that Howard Carter was the famous archeologist who discovered King Tut's tomb. His class was preparing for biography day, and each student had to choose a famous person in American history to research. Brent insisted on being Howard Carter and wouldn't take no for an answer. His teacher agreed but only if Brent could come up with at least one book about Howard by the next day. After our two-minute conversation he jumped on his bike and rode all the way to the library by himself. He came home with four books, and you guessed ... he was Howard Carter for biography day. Mrs. Kirchoff grew to love Brent, and when he was ill, she brought him several books about Egypt. We still have them!

6 My Social Life: Bike Riding, Basketball Camp, and Piano Lessons

For physical training is of some value, but godliness has value for all things, holding promise for both the present life and the life to come.

—1 Timothy 4:8

Brent on his skateboard wearing a red shirt

In fifth grade I had my first male teacher. His name was Mr. Brents. I don't know if this was an accident or on purpose, but there was a Brent in Mr. Brent's class. Every Friday we had a class meeting. I *love* world history! It's so interesting to me. I think school is great, although sometimes it gets overwhelming. I love the town I live in. It's a great town. It has great schools, a nice library, tasty places to eat, and wonderful people. I was in a couple of basketball leagues at the park district. My mom always signed us up to get all five of us out of the house to give her a break. I was also in tennis and soccer and took piano lessons.

Bike riding became one of Brent's favorite activities, eventually. It seemed to take him forever to learn how to ride his bike. He was very adventurous in some ways, and then in others he held himself back. Bill had run around the block with him for several years, trying to teach Brent to learn to ride his bike without training wheels. Both Nick and Justin were riding without help, so I decided to take matters into my own hands. I knew that kids would eventually start making fun of him and I was confident that he could do it, so I grounded him to his bike for one hour. I told him that he had to be on his bike the entire time and that it would be his choice to either sit there on the driveway or to actually try to ride it. I also let him know that I was not going to help him. I went inside the house and set the timer. Before I knew it, he was riding his bike up and down the sidewalk. He was *so excited* and thanked me for forcing him to try. Not only was bike riding great for the boys, but it was also the best thing for me. It was difficult to interrupt nap time and the importance of a routine for the younger ones, so weather permitting, the older boys rode their bikes to their different activities. Each week they would ride to the park district for soccer or basketball, to the library for fun, and to piano lessons at Mrs. Price's house.

An out-of-school activity that I do is a program called Son Light Express. It's a church group at my home church for sixth, seventh, and eighth graders. One of my friends that I hang out with the most is Jonathan, who lives right down the street from me. There was another Jonathan that lived by us, but he moved. Before that, we would always play capture the flag at each other's houses.

—

A few days before school started each year, the class lists were posted on doors of the main entrance to the building. As soon as we heard the news that the lists were ready to view, a ride to the school on our bikes was in order. A new teacher was added to the fifth-grade team, and his name just happened to be Mr. Brents. Brent was delighted to be in his class. Fifth grade was exciting and fun, but nothing compared to sixth grade. Again we raced over to the school once we learned that the lists were hung. Brent was in Mrs. McHugh's homeroom. We had a *blast* with her name; we called her Mrs. Mc-*huge*. Although school was always something Brent looked forward to, this year was his favorite by far. He loved learning about world history in social studies and enjoyed his LA/LIT class with Mrs. McHugh. Brent's personality and character began to shine, and he made an impression on everyone he met. Mr. Roy had the privilege of teaching Brent his favorite subject and was so impressed with his cartoons that he kept most of Brent's drawings on his bulletin board for years.

Jonah with Geppetto and Pinocchio in the whale drawn by Brent

7

Talents: That Was My Part

For it is God who works in you to will and to act in order to fulfill his good purpose.

—Philippians 2:13

Brent dressed in his Egyptian outfit

Some of my special talents are acting, making comics, and playing video games. Ever since second grade, I have taken piano lessons. I still take them. When I was in basketball at the park district, my team was losing, and there were only five seconds on the clock. I got the ball, shot, and made a three-pointer in the last couple of seconds. Another time I had the ball, and I was being guarded by a hyper kid. He swung at the ball but missed and swiped my glasses right off my face. He backed away from me because he was so shocked. Then, without my glasses, I shot the ball into a big blur. I made the shot.

—

Brent loved being in school, and he also loved being a big brother. Our family was like a well-oiled machine. We all worked together, and everyone had their special chore: Brent would dust, Nick would vacuum the stairs, Justin would help sort laundry, Kevin was the recycle guy, and Corrina would help get the mail. Perfect! Many times when someone would call the house, they would say, "Oh, I'll call back. It sounds like you're having a party." We did have lots of parties, but usually it was just us. Things were hardly ever quiet, and I *never* had a chance to get bored. Dinner time was my favorite, and sometimes things would get so out of hand I just had to join in on it. Imagine all the fun four boys could create while sitting around the dinner table.

Yet there were times I would find myself completely overwhelmed and physically exhausted by the responsibility of raising five unique and energetic children. And there are things that I just don't remember, like Kevin or Corrina's first birthdays. I know they each had one, but I couldn't tell you how we celebrated. Hopefully someday I will find pictures to remind me. I'm sure Bill felt overwhelmed by the responsibility of providing for all of us. He worked a lot and would come home exhausted, but he never complained. Our everyday life's circumstances were not always perfect, but somehow God always came through. We had other struggles, as most families do. Things weren't trouble-free, but our perspective on life was simple: enjoy each moment and celebrate absolutely everything. Jesus was my rock and was always close to me. Whenever I needed His assurance, I felt His love and power come over me until …

I'm not exactly sure when or for how long, but God began to be quiet in my life. I still studied His word, went to church, and even prayed, but I felt like He wasn't there. I began to wonder if all this "Christian" stuff was really real. I searched, prayed, and began to question everything. I started to feel frustrated and hoped that He would show Himself to me like He had in the past and still nothing. I was so confused. I'd never heard of God being quiet/silent in someone's life. I was afraid to share my struggles with my friends because I didn't understand what was happening. I was under the impression that if I *loved* God and did my best in all that He asked, my life would be like a perfect picture—painted on a perfect canvas, a work of art for all to see. I imagined that painting had beautiful color, balance, and texture. In reality what I was experiencing was just the opposite: flat, colorless, chaotic, and empty. I had no idea that He was preparing me for the events to come.

What I remember most about the summer of 2001 is swimming and screaming. Brent just finished sixth grade in school, Nick fourth, and Justin second, and Kevin was about to begin kindergarten. Corrina was now three and I was finally feeling better. My pregnancy with her took a huge toll on my body. I would get winded often and had breathing episodes at night while sleeping if I did too much during the day. We spent lots of time at Oma's house swimming in her pool. What great fun for kids of all ages, including me. Sometimes I actually felt guilty because I was enjoying the pool with the kids while Bill was out working so hard. His job continued to be demanding, and he took advantage of every minute that was made available for him to work. Often I felt like a single parent. I did appreciate his commitment to provide and still do; but the kids began to notice he was gone a lot. During dinner one evening while he was home, one of the kids prayed that Daddy be safe, just like we always did … except this time he was there. He was shaken and said, "Hey, guys, I'm here." I think that struck a nerve in Bill's heart.

By now Brent was on his way to becoming a teenager, and he wasn't exactly thrilled about taking his medicine. I'm embarrassed to admit it, but most days I would end up screaming at him. There were even times during the day when I'd have to call my dad to come over to get Brent to take his meds. Rejection was right around the corner if Brent didn't comply. Even this far out from his transplant, we still had to be extremely careful to prevent it from happening. I tried to get him to understand what all his meds were and how they worked to protect his heart. When he wouldn't cooperate, I would freak out, leaving all of us a bit crazy.

Over the years Brent constantly begged me to let him swim in the lake, or ocean, as he called it when he was little. I rarely gave in. We had access to the pool every summer. My parents, who lived three blocks away, kept their pool open for us to use. Still there was something that drew Brent to the "ocean." A couple weeks before his seventh-grade school year was to start, I agreed to let the three older boys go tubing on Bangs Lake with our family friends. They had a *blast*. To hear their stories when they got home and feel their excitement, I felt confident that nothing bad would happen. Just days after the fun, white pus began to literally fill both of Brent's ear canals. Immediately I brought him to see our pediatrician. Shortly after Brent was born, I had the privilege of meeting her, and she became his primary medical caregiver and partnered with the hospital downtown and learned all she could about keeping Brent and the rest of our kids healthy and safe. Puzzled by this infection, she tried everything she could think of, yet nothing was working. At the same time, Brent's heart rate was elevated. Every time Brent got an infection or was about to become, sick his heart rate would rise. I was a bit concerned but not panicked about his heart, because he clearly had an infection but in his ears. I was deeply worried, and so was our pediatrician. A few years earlier he had a terrible case of strep throat that would not clear up. As a last-ditch effort, he was treated with IV antibiotics. Thankfully that worked. This time I felt like we were on the same road, only the infection lasted a lot longer. The balance of keeping Brent's immune system sleepy enough to prevent rejection and awake enough to fight this infection was proving itself tricky. We visited the office several more times, and after four weeks of no results, she referred us to an ENT specialist downtown. To be on the safe side, she also scheduled an echo of his heart.

Brent was so mad that he was going to miss school that he pouted the whole ride to Chicago. By now my heart was heavy, and I insisted that Bill come too. He took the day off work and drove us to the hospital. Our first appointment was with the ENT doctor. Unfortunately, our favorite ENT specialist was not available to see us that day, so we were seen by another doctor. He was very professional, kind, and confused ... because when he looked in Brent's ears, the infection was completely gone! *Impossible!* We had just been at the pediatrician's office the day before and things looked horrible. The doctor was so concerned about his ears that she scheduled an emergency appointment downtown while we were waiting in her office. I wasn't sure what to think. How could this be? I prayed like crazy the entire night before and the entire ride there but found no comfort. Then we had our echo. I was not worried in the least. I couldn't wait to get back on the road and head back home. During the echocardiogram, I wasn't sure the ultrasound tech knew what she was doing because the echo seemed to take forever. She was new; we'd never seen her there before, and I was feeling impatient. Finally Brent's echo was finished. Now just a quick visit with the cardiologist and then back home.

It was tense and quiet while we waited for the cardiologist to show up. I was still confused about Brent's ears and irritated that we had to wait so long to see the cardiologist. Brent was obviously annoyed that he had missed school, and I know Bill felt like I was overreacting to the whole ear infection thing. Then without much warning, the cardiologist burst into the exam room, and I was taken back by his careless and sloppy entry.

He slammed Brent's oversized chart down on the examining table and shouted, "Well, these hearts don't last forever!"

I felt like I was in the middle of a heavyweight boxing match, *bam*, a hit to the right, *bam*, and a knockout punch to the left. My ears ringing, I just stared at the doctor, not believing what he just said. Bill quickly excused the two of them into the hallway and reminded the doctor that Brent was a twelve-year-old boy who deserved to be talked to in a more professional and respectable way. When they both returned to the room, I insisted that the echo tech made a mistake and that her echo was the problem, not Brent's heart. No chance; Brent's heart was not functioning properly, and a full study was needed immediately. It was scheduled for the first thing the next morning. Talk about confused. We went to Chicago because Brent had been fighting a visible double ear infection for weeks, and now that was all clear. *How?* Then within minutes we find out that his heart was not functioning properly, and he needed to have a biopsy and heart cath right away. Can't be possible … he ran a mile in gym the day before. I was back to not being able to breathe. My head was spinning, and my heart was racing. My biggest fear was about to come true. I don't remember much of the ride home, nor do I remember the time we spent there. I was in total shock, pleading, "God, where are you? Please can You hear me? *I need You now.* If You are real, please, please, please … nothing."

Brent was so nervous about having a heart study. Although he was young when he had had his last study, he remembered what they were like and gave me full details about it. Listening to him retell his experience was painful for me to listen to. He was three years old when he had his last full biopsy and heart cath. We decided to stop biopsies and heart caths unless other tests that were less invasive proved that there was a need for it. There was a need for it now and the next day, Bill and I found ourselves sitting in the OR waiting room again. Trying to find something to keep my mind off of what was happening was almost impossible. While my ears were still ringing from the beating the day before and my heart wildly pounding, I was desperately praying for good news. I'll never forget when the nurse came out to let us know that Brent had transplant coronary disease (TCAD). All my breathing stopped. My heart stopped, and this time I didn't care if I fell apart or not. Rejection and infection were our enemies, but we knew that transplant coronary disease would be our worst nightmare. The pain of those words was so deep I couldn't breathe. I just sat there with tears pouring from the depth my heart, and that's when Jesus showed up. Yes, right there, in full power and stronger than ever. His Spirit completely filled me and took my next breath and has taken every single one with me since October 17, 2001, the day Brent was diagnosed with TCAD. Strange as this may sound, my immediate thoughts were of Nicholas, Justin, Kevin, and Corrina. I desperately needed to be there for them now more than ever!

We had to wait for more than an hour before we could see Brent after the devastating diagnosis. While we were waiting for him to come out of recovery, the transplant team strongly encouraged us to consider putting him on the list for a second transplant. It was only yesterday that we were downtown for an ear infection, and now he needed a new heart? Back up … rewrite this part of the story. Wake up from this horrible nightmare, and yet at the same time I was filled with *peace.* Question after question … no complete answers. Up to this point, only two patients treated had been retransplanted for TCD. The odds did not look good. One patient was diagnosed with the disease only two months after his second transplant, and the other patient was about to celebrate his year anniversary. We were told that the chance of getting a healthy heart were not good. Brent was now the size of an average adult, and healthy adult hearts were hard to find. They also told us to expect rejection to be a common threat as a match was not a top priority. Finding any available heart was. His new heart, if that is what we were going to decide, would most likely be too large for his body as well, causing strain on his already struggling kidneys. This news came hard. Brent had never rejected his heart. His biggest struggle was keeping infection at bay. Overall we were winning that fight, and the thought of adding rejection, a potential sick heart, kidney strain, and the possibility of getting TCD again only made things seem hopeless. TCD had always been a threat. We had always expected that by the time Brent ever faced this disease, a cure or successful treatment option would have been discovered. There were many speculations as to why this disease occurred. One was that the anti-rejection medication, which is necessary to keep the transplanted heart healthy, actually caused this disease. Another theory was that TCD was a form of rejection that was not yet preventable or predictable and was always fatal. Preventing it from happening at all was not only devastating to patients and their families, but it was frustrating to the medical team as well. Being informed about TCAD, we decided to give medication therapy a try. As far as we knew, this treatment option was not a guarantee but was worth attempting. Brent would now be adding several medications to his daily schedule, and even if he were to have the second transplant, he would have to continue with these drugs for the rest of his life.

Walking into Brent's room after his biopsy was extremely difficult. He was super mad and I think mostly scared. "Why did you let them do this to me?" were his exact words. It was like a time warp bringing me back to the ICU when as an infant his eyes said the exact same thing. This time I pleaded with the Lord to heal him and to give him strength. Deep in my heart all I kept hearing was, "I know what's happening. Trust Me. I'm taking him home." Peace that cannot be explained, that only comes from the Lord, was my comfort.

During that time Bill and I devoted ourselves to being consistent in praying for Brent's health, our marriage, and Nicholas, Justin, Kevin, and Corrina. I'm sure life was very confusing to them, but at the time, I had no energy or strength to even notice. Yes, they were all heavy on my heart, but the urgency of Brent's needs filled my days and nights. Jesus was our strength and even more so for Brent. When we got the news that Brent had a 90 percent blocked left coronary artery, emergency treatments were scheduled for the next day. Again, we were able to go home for the night, and this time I clearly remember having a family dinner. My sister-in law made us dinner. We had pasta with sausage and added orange juice to drink. Somehow that seemed odd, the orange juice, but that's what everyone wanted to drink. The kids laughed and carried on, as they always did. Meal time at the Vaughans' always felt like a party. Yet this night Brent was quiet as he knew we would be heading back to a new hospital again the next morning. Bill and I were numb.

It was October 18, 2001. Since Brent was of adult size, the treatment to open the blockage in his heart would require him to be treated in a hospital that takes care of adults. I still can't pass that place without losing it. Our experience there was less than adequate. In my opinion, I would call it horrible. The cardiologist who was responsible for taking care of Brent wasn't exactly comforting. He may have been the best doctor for the job, but he left both Bill and me scared out of our minds. He wouldn't answer our questions clearly, and I wouldn't accept anything less than clear. Before any procedure, we were always informed about the treatment. We were used to our doctors, who would clearly describe the risks/benefits, and they would always do their best to reassure us as Brent's parents. This time the doctor wouldn't even look us in the eye. I needed some encouragement or reassurance that things would be okay. All he kept saying is that Brent might have an electrical problem during the procedure, while looking at the floor. I felt like I was talking to a teenager with a huge attitude problem. *What* was he trying to say? I kept thinking, *What does that mean?* Several times he repeated that there may be an electrical problem during the procedure. He acted as if we were keeping him from an important game of golf and that he didn't have time to spend talking to this kid's parents. He'd roll his eyes and huffed and puffed, and by now I wanted to blow him down.

Finally I said, "Please just say it clearly. We need to know what we might be facing."

He said there was a 50 percent chance that Brent would die during this procedure. His blockage had some complications, and he was not sure what to expect until the stents were put in place. Well, that was reassuring—*not*! How could we sign the consent to allow this doctor who couldn't even look us in the eye and who had absolutely no compassion to work on our son? I asked him what he would do if he were in our shoes, and with all his arrogant self, he boldly looked me in the eyes and proclaimed that he would never be in my shoes. (Hope he's still right.) To that I asked him if I could pray for him before he took Brent to the operating room.

Shocked and irritated, he said in a sarcastic voice, "I'm not going to pray."

I told him that I needed to pray for him, and so I did right there out loud and thanked God for this man. The next hour or however long we waited for Brent felt like an entire lifetime. Yes, I could sense God's presence was still with me, but I couldn't sit still. I couldn't wrap my mind around the fact that Brent was having stents put into his heart while awake and at any moment he could die. When he finally came back into the room, I never left his side. I held his hand and just looked at him. I was so thankful that he was alive. The fight was not over. The stents could shift, the other arteries could close off, and the transplant disease could continue to spread. We left the hospital the next day with our son and a whole new regimen of medications. And guess what just happened to show up just minutes before we were going to be discharged? The puss.

Again feeling panicked because I wanted so desperately to leave the hospital and go home, I quickly called our pediatrician and scheduled an appointment to see someone in the office on our way home. Hoping that the new team of doctors would be satisfied, they agreed to let us go even with this impending infection. Now we were on a quest to find out what was happening in Brent's ears. This time, things were a bit more complicated because he was on so much more medication. He went from taking meds seven times a day to taking meds twenty-one times a day. I'm so thankful for my sister Pam, who took the time to create an Excel spreadsheet and researched every single drug Brent was taking. She helped me create a schedule that was doable. We had to make sure that none of the meds he needed for his heart would be adversely affected by the new antibiotic we were hoping to add to clear up his ears. After our visit to the pediatrician's office, I am so thankful we had an appointment secured with our favorite ENT specialist in Westchester the next day.

It felt so good to be home, but Brent's care seemed overwhelming. The rest of the kids were definitely there, and I could tell they needed me. After dinner Brent seemed troubled and asked to talk privately. He sat me down on the couch and told me not to freak out. He was feeling chest pain and was very scared. I was puzzled since we were told that he would never be able to feel chest pain because the nerves to his heart were cut during his transplant.

Before I could say anything, he grabbed my hand, looked me in the eye, and said, "If something bad happens, it's not your fault. I've seen you take care of me. It's not my fault either. It's no one's fault. This is just something that happened." Then he asked me the unimaginable: "Am I going to die?" Being hopeful that the medications we were trying would work and having a peace beyond anything I could ever imagine, I felt confident that things would be okay.

A quick prayer and the words just flowed: "Brent, we're all going to die. We just don't know when."

To that he said, "Well, I just want to make the most of the time I have left." I was completely taken back by his words of courage. I was thrilled when I called the transplant team because they were certain that everything was fine and that we could rest comfortably at home.

Nothing could have been better than to see the ENT specialist the next day. We had so much confidence in him. He could be described as the Mr. Rodgers of medicine—not in a bad way, in the best possible way ever. He was so professional, qualified, skilled, and compassionate. He not only helped parents feel at ease, but he was also amazing with children. He was calm, respectful, and just the kind of person you'd want to take care of your son or daughter. We'd been seeing him for years. Brent consistently had trouble with his inner ears when he was younger, and Justin did as well. We were thankful for his care and his bedside manner. The trouble in Brent's ears proved to be more than just a simple fix. The puss was cultured, and thankfully a suitable antibiotic was found that would not interfere with the rest of his heart meds. Not only did we need to give Brent the meds, but he also needed to have his ears professionally cleaned two times a week. I continued to drive Brent to Westchester, white knuckling it the whole way, until his ears were clear. A new concern was that this infection had spread to Brent's jawbone because he was feeling pain in his jaw. Waiting for the results of the CAT scan was difficult. If the infection had spread to his bone, Brent would have needed surgery to remove the infected bone immediately. This type of infection was hard to treat in patients with normal immune systems. One little trip to the ocean was playing in my mind. I almost kissed the doctor and the floor of the room we were in when we got the news, thankfully, that the infection had not spread. We were hopeful and pleased when the antibiotics began to work. Brent's immune system was now on high suppression. We were learning all over again the key to keeping infection at bay and rejection away and desperately praying for TCAD to clear.

The full impact of Brent's last nine months and remarkable journey was not witnessed by many. Most people did not understand or know of his condition. He basically stopped going to school shortly after his diagnosis in October. Not only were we busy at hospitals and appointments, but Brent also was no longer the energetic kid he once was. He would try to go to school, and after a full day, he would spend the rest of the week at home in bed, completely exhausted. His body had a difficult time adjusting to his new meds. Feeding him was almost impossible. He was so disappointed because life as a middle school student was exciting to him. He enjoyed his classes, loved laughing with his friends, and finally had the chance to be in a school play. When he was younger, he would often be selected for a speaking part in the school musicals. Brent loved to perform. I remember asking him if he felt nervous when he was up in front of others. He confidently replied, "Not at all. I'm just myself cause if I'm not then I'll look like a jerk." I can only think of one time that Brent lost it in front of a crowd. Bill and I were always whooping it up with the kids. Brent, Nick, and Justin were all taking piano lessons, and they had their annual piano recital. On the way to the church the day of the performance, Bill and I were teasing Brent because he was going to play "Singing in the Rain." We told him that once he started playing, Bill and I would stand up, pop open the umbrella and sing along. Oh, how we all laughed ... except Brent. Of course we were just kidding, but Brent obviously had no idea. He was so nervous that he messed up and had to start his song over twice. Bill and I both felt awful. We learned our lesson.

We proudly celebrated the fact that Brent got a part in the middle school play. Unfortunately, after his surgery he could no longer handle going to school for a full day, so we tried to send him for half days. This still proved to be too much. His drama coach and the school administration suggested that he come to rehearsals and continue in the play even though the rules stated that if you missed any part of a school day, you would not be allowed to go to practice. If you missed three rehearsals, you would not be allowed to perform. Brent appreciated the offer but didn't think that bending the rules was fair to the other students, so he willingly gave up his part. The weekend of the performance, Brent insisted on being there the opening night. I gladly took him but felt that overwhelming sorrow. Shortly after the lights were dimmed and the curtains were drawn, the play began.

Brent leaned over and whispered in my ear while he was pointing on stage, "Mom, that was my part."

I quietly cried a river. Sadness and *amazement* filled my heart as I watched my son "make the most of the time he had left." He continued to smile, laugh, and applaud. He ended up going to all three performances. He was genuinely happy! That peace and happiness could only have come from God.

Thanksgiving of 2001 was days away, and so was Brent's first echo since his diagnosis. If the meds and his stents were working properly, his heart function should have returned to normal. As far as I could tell, things were improving. His vitals were stable, and all his medication levels were right on. His ears were finally clearing from the infection. The echo tech didn't take as long as the last time, and we were thrilled to learn that Brent's heart function was back to normal. Talk about being thankful. Peace still ruled in my heart, and I still had this secure confidence that all would be well, no matter what. To keep Brent's heart healthy and to fend off the further spread of TCAD, we were scheduled for more testing the week before Christmas. Gary, the echo tech who had been seeing Brent since he was born, insisted on doing his stress test. We felt confident that we were going to continue to get good news. As we were walking out of the stress lab, Gary once again insisted on walking with us. I knew something was wrong when our eyes met and his were filled with tears. He didn't have to say a word. We knew. He hugged us all, and we said our good-byes. That was the last time we saw Gary.

Brent's heart function was no longer normal, and TCAD was spreading. There was no way to know how quickly or how much time Brent had left.

We called our church and asked them to continue to pray—to pray for a miracle, for wisdom, and for strength. We decided to wait until after Christmas to share the news with Brent. We wanted him to be able to celebrate this holiday with all the joy a boy his age should. We even hosted a New Year's Eve party for Brent and several of his friends. I followed him around the house with my camera, taking as many pictures as I could, and I know he got annoyed. He came up to me in the kitchen and said, "I know what you're doing."

To that I asked, "Is it wrong?" He thought about it for a minute answered no and then got himself ready and posed for a picture. It's my favorite picture of him.

Christmas was over, and we had just started a brand-new year. It was now time to tell Brent that the medication treatments we were using were not working. We sought wisdom from the elders of our church, and it was suggested that we do this during a family meeting. Bill and I were both sobbing and unable to talk, yet somehow, we got the point across. Brent just looked at us and asked us why we were crying.

At first I didn't think he understood what we had said, until he quietly whispered, "Oh, I get it. It's gonna be hard for you when I'm gone."

To that he again said that he was going to make the most of the time he had left. Feeling so guilty and ashamed for screaming at him the summer before he was diagnosed, I felt like I needed to apologize for being so hard on him. I told Brent that I was sorry for screaming at him.

He said, "Hey, no problem. That's what kids do. They fight with their parents … if it wasn't my medicine it would have been something else." I try to remember that now, especially when I'm having trouble with the others.

For some reason people had the idea that we were keeping all of Brent's medical news a secret to him. To those on the outside, having a second transplant seemed like an easy thing to do. There was absolutely no peace in that decision, and the three of us (Brent, Bill, and I) felt confident that God was with us the whole time. Someone actually called the hospital transplant nurse and told them that we weren't telling Brent the whole truth about his condition. This same person suspected that we were being neglectful and wanted to take Brent away from us because in their eyes we were seen as unfit parents. Bam, bam. Wasn't it enough to get knocked out with the devastating news, but now while we were down and out, *bam,* more hits. Shocked and disgusted, we did our best to ignore the threats and rumors going around. Neighborhood gossip fests delighted in sharing our story, and I remember one mom boldly telling me how she didn't agree with our decision as we waited for the bus to take our children to school. I just looked at her deeply confused and reminded her that she should be glad it wasn't her decision to make. End of conversation. I didn't feel the need to explain the details, but I was feeling *very lonely* and hurt.

Enjoying the time he had left was Brent's mission. To make sure he was informed of his condition, the transplant team called us in for a meeting to openly discuss his treatment and Brent's options. Feeling angry and overwhelmed, I regret that I allowed them to try to scare Brent into a second transplant. The cardiologist proceeded to display the results of Brent's last cath on a large screen so we could all see the TCAD, which was spreading. He quickly announced that Brent would have a heart attack at any moment without warning and that the heart attack would be fatal. He also told Brent that healthy hearts were not easy to find and that a sick heart would be better than dying. He also told Brent that he needed to make a decision and to make it quickly.

He asked Brent if he clearly understood that he was dying and to that Brent replied, "Yes, and I'm not afraid." When we left the meeting, Bill had to use the washroom. While Brent and I were waiting for Bill, Brent looked at me and said, "I have four words for you: *no way—exclamation point!*"

From that point on, Brent made goals for himself. One of the goals he set was to be able to start eighth grade with the rest of his classmates. He hadn't been in school for a very long time but felt like he was ready for the challenge. Since he was still on all the medications, we decided to have Brent home schooled. He was allowed to have a tutor come and work with him at home. When he found out that he was going to have a tutor, he had a fit. He clearly wanted to let everyone know that he was not stupid and that the tutor was not necessary. I explained that the tutor was only a liason, someone who would bring his schoolwork back and forth. Beth proved to be the best thing. Not only did she bring Brent's assignments, but she also brought a friendly smile, encouragement, and treats. They were not just for Brent either; Nicholas, Justin, Kevin, and Corrina were being spoiled too.

8 My Future My Greatest Wish

"For I know the plans I have for you," declares the Lord, "plans to prosper you and not to harm you, plans to give you hope and a future."

—Jeremiah 29:11 NIV

Brent with his siblings standing on the pool deck in their swimming suits

When I get older, I want to go to college and take classes on Egyptology. Right now I have a paper route every Wednesday. When I grow up, I want to be an archaeologist. When I grow up, I want to stay right here in my hometown, although I'll be traveling a lot because of my job. As a side job (because sometimes archaeologists do not earn a lot of money), I'll work as a professor at a college. The college will hopefully help pay for my archaeological expeditions.

———

"I'm the luckiest mommy," was something I said a lot! Whenever any of my kids would ask me what I would wish for if I could only have one wish, I would *always* say that my greatest wish would be that we would all stay healthy. At that time nothing else mattered.

The company that Bill was working for needed him to travel, and the demands on his time away from our family was proving to add more stress than we could bear. He decided to quit his job in February, mostly because we were told that Brent's time was short. Not long after he quit, they contacted Bill to continue providing service to their customers. Bill not only started the service department, but he was also solely responsible for servicing the air pollution equipment for their customers. This provided some income for our family, and I also went back to substitute teaching. I started the 2001–2002 year, excited to get back to work outside the home. Brent, Nick, and Justin had always asked me to work at their schools. When school time started in the fall of 2001, I had everything in place: a sitter for Corrina and Kevin and the ability to work when I could. Substitute teaching was flexible, and I needed that. Once Brent was diagnosed with TCAD, it was necessary for me to stay at home, so I took my name off the subbing list. Early in the spring of 2002, Brent's condition was stable, and I decided to try subbing again. It just so happened that I walked into a perfect situation. They needed a part-time sub afternoons for a first-grade teacher on maternity leave. I worked Monday through Friday from 12:00 to 3:40 p.m. I enjoyed that time away from the house. It felt good because I was able to be creative and productive and the extra money was helpful. The school was aware of Brent's condition and agreed to hire me even if I had to leave. Bill was feeling productive as well. His service company was started, and he consistently found work to keep busy. His plans to continue the business were sketchy, planning our future was not something we were capable of doing at that time.

Overall our family was doing as well as we could. I don't think Justin, Kevin, or Corrina fully understood what was happening. Nicholas was always quiet and more mature than the rest of his classmates, but he started to withdraw at home and I didn't even notice. He was devastated when we shared the news about Brent's heart and immediately he asked if he could give Brent his heart. I'll never forget him saying that. Meanwhile Brent continued to set goals and was thrilled when he finished all the schoolwork necessary to start eighth grade that coming fall. It still amazes me that he did. Not only did he set that goal, but he also started the countdowns for the next movie, game, or book that was about to be released. We all looked forward to the upcoming events just as much as he did but felt a deep sorrow when the particular event would pass. Oh, I still do not know how we endured that time. All I can say is that God was there every step of the way. To walk hand in hand with your child through the valley has got to be the most difficult of all life's experiences. Did I say that I wanted to change God's story?

Trying to keep the other four kids quiet and not wild proved itself a battle we were losing. Brent tried really hard to keep up with the rest of the bunch but often felt overwhelmed and wanted things calm. Most nights Brent would ask me to drive him to Walmart, so the two of us would head out just as the others went to bed. He never really wanted to buy anything; he just liked getting out of the house. We would secretly hold hands in the car just like we did every time I'd have to take him to the hospital for a blood draw. I remember our last road trip was the evening before he died. I had forgotten to pick up Brent's meds earlier that day, so as we were driving to the store, I asked if he wanted to wait in the car or come in with me. While I was paying, he sat quietly watching from the row of chairs near the counter.

We left the store, and as soon as we got into the car, he looked at me and said, "Thanks for never making me feel guilty about having to get my medicine. I just realized how much extra I have been to you and Dad my whole life."

I looked him in the eyes and said, "Your meds are not extra. They are needs, like food and clothes."

Brent interrupted me and said, "Mom, I have three brothers and a sister, and you've never had to do all this for them." I tried to explain again, but he insisted that he was right and would only accept a "you're welcome."

By now Brent was feeling uneasy about sleeping at home. He would get aggravated that the others were so wild and noisy, and he knew that his time was growing short. He decided to sleep at my parents' house just in case. Looking back now, I can't believe I let him. I never wanted to be apart from him, but in so many ways that was the best thing for all of us. I needed a break, and the kids needed to be kids. On July 17, 2002, at 9:00 a.m., I got a call from my mom. Brent had started throwing up and wouldn't stop. I quickly called my sister-in-law to see if she could come get Corrina. Kevin and Justin went to go play at a friend's house, and Nick stayed with my parents. I set up the basement for Brent so he could rest quietly. He had a migraine headache and was able to get comfortable on the couch, where it was dark, cool, and quiet. Before he came home, I was on the phone with the transplant nurse, and she suggested that we see our local pediatrician. Ear infections were common, and he had been having headaches a lot lately. Early in the week I had taken Brent to see the eye doctor just to make sure his headaches weren't due to his eyes; they weren't. When we visited the pediatrician, she was concerned, as we all were, and suggested that we have an ultrasound of Brent's gallbladder. In the past few weeks she had seen several patients who were on long-term medications who were now suffering from gallbladder problems. Without delay she had an appointment scheduled immediately for us at our local hospital.

Since Brent was now adult size, I was not able to join him in the men's dressing room or the lab. Thankfully, Bill was able to be with him, and the test seemed to take forever. The results were immediate. Brent's gallbladder had a strange covering and one of his kidneys had developed a cyst, but the main concern at this point was that he had a small amount of fluid in both his lungs. Feeling confident that a few days in the hospital would clear things up, we were now heading home to get our things and travel to Chicago.

When we arrived at home, I called the church and asked if they would pray. I also asked if we could reschedule Brent's meeting with the pastor. Brent had wanted to be baptized when he was around seven. When he was young, I had always suggested that he wait until he was older to make sure he understood his decision to follow Christ. He continued to ask over the years, and now that he was ill, we happily agreed. For Brent to be baptized, he needed to meet with the pastor to make sure he understood what his decision meant. Nick and Justin met with the pastor earlier in the week. Since Brent wasn't feeling well that day, we scheduled a private meeting in our home. The pastor agreed that he would pray and that he would find a better time to meet with Brent. Over the course of his illness, Brent's focus was not so much on himself as it was on others. He was especially concerned for the salvation of family and friends. One day he told me that he took care of business with Kevin and Corrina. He actually led them to Christ. My hero!

While we were at home gathering our things, Nick stopped by to get his supplies ready for the long-dreaded job of the paper route. Brent laughed at him, and the two of them joked while Nick was rolling papers with my dad. We all said our good-byes but never realized that would be the last. Just before we left, Brent actually said that he was hungry. What a huge surprise. Hungry was a word that Brent hardly ever said. I wasn't sure what to do. I didn't know if feeding him would be allowed since we were on our way to being admitted to the hospital. I decided to call the pediatrician's office. I tried twice. No luck; couldn't get through. Then I decided to call the hospital downtown. I tried two times as well and without any luck again. Bill and I decided that if Brent was hungry, we should get him some food. When we asked what he wanted, he *boldly* exclaimed, *"Ribs."* Typically we fed him anything he wanted. However, he'd been sick all day, and with his heart condition, we strongly encouraged him to make a different choice. That's when he suggested crab legs. I agreed and Bill just looked at me like I was crazy, but I felt confident this was the right thing to do.

Earlier that summer we celebrated my birthday at a Chinese all-you-can-eat buffet. I remembered that they had crab legs. We decided to go to the same place as the restaurant was on the way to the hospital. Brent and I stayed in the car while Bill went in to check and see how crowded the place was and if they had crab legs. The place was empty. They had just reopened for dinner, and the crowds had not yet come. Indeed, they had a heaping tray of piping hot crab legs just waiting for us.

Before Bill got back to the car, Brent looked at me and said, "I get the whole God thing."

Filled with peace beyond anything I've ever felt, I told him how glad I was. Then we went in to eat our last supper. Brent was weak and asked if we could get him his plate of food. Bill loaded Brent's plate with a heaping pile of crab legs. Brent's eyes were delighted, and he struggled to crack the first leg in half. Bill helped, and then with much enthusiasm, Brent placed the meat in his mouth. His smile was from ear to ear.

It was obvious that he was pleased, and he proudly announced, "This is my last supper, just like Jesus, except I'm breaking crab legs instead."

Funny Brent. My mind was still full of laughter. As we were driving to the restaurant, Brent decided to name all the things he could think of that had to do with corn. The farm fields we passed were bursting, and the corn was more than knee deep. Corn, corndogs, corn bread, candy corn … Oh we had a blast. Corn on the cob, corn beef, corn nuts … and the laughter continued. Not realizing what was taking place, we again broke out in laughter when Brent opened his fortune cookie and tried desperately to trade it with either Bill's or mine. His fortune said, "Soon you will be crossing the great waters." We both laughed and said, "Fat chance." As we were leaving the restaurant, Brent recognized that we were close to where Bill's brother lived. He asked if we could go say good-bye to Corrina. We did. I'll never forget him hugging her.

When we arrived at the hospital, the emergency room was our entrance in because it was after hours. The cardiologist on call was someone new. We'd never met her before, so I was feeling a bit apprehensive, and the triage nurse wasn't exactly pleasant. I tried to explain Brent's condition and told her that it was not safe for Brent to hang around in the ER waiting room for fear of contracting another infection. She was obviously having a bad day, so I explained to her that once they had a suitable room for Brent, they would be able to find us in the main lobby area. Since it was after hours, no one would be there. As we were walking down the hallway to the main lobby, this beautiful and kind woman introduced herself.

"Hi, my name is Kendra; you must be the Vaughans. I've been waiting for you."

She quickly brought us to the isolation room in the ER and proceeded to check Brent's vitals. Next she did an echo. Tears filled her eyes, and she was sorry to tell us that things looked worse than expected. The laughter had all but stopped, and Brent was feeling very uncomfortable.

He looked at me and said, "They always do more than they say."

I assured him that we would only agree to IV fluids and noninvasive testing. He agreed, and he began to relax. There was one more experimental drug that we were considering trying to stop this TCAD. We were told that the side effect of this drug was a definite case of lymphoma, and we would cross that bridge if we came to it. We didn't want Brent to be the first patient to try this drug, and we were hopeful and waiting on results from another family who found themselves in our same situation. I don't think they started the treatment for the same reasons we were reluctant to, but since we were in the hospital, we decided to go ahead a give it a try. This medication was extremely powerful and was given only in IV form. It was also given in ICU, and the patient would require extensive observation. We were expecting to be in the hospital for at least three but no longer than five days. The fluid in Brent's lungs was still a huge concern to Dr. Kendra. To transfer Brent to his room in ICU, a chest x-ray was needed. The nurse thought he was stable enough to walk to the x-ray department. Bill waited in the isolation room, and Brent and I walked together. Within a few steps and before my very eyes, he became weak and needed to sit down, and then he was gone! His eyes were fully opened, and his color was dark, just like the first day of his life. Nothing—no pulse, no breathing, nothing. The nurse who walked with us frantically tried to call a code. I was screaming for Bill. I kept asking the nurse to get my husband. I didn't want to be alone. I knew that he would have wanted to be there too. Then in an instant I saw a rush of life literally pour back into Brent. Thankful and shocked, I asked him if he was okay.

All he said was, "Yeah that was weird."

Within seconds we were now in the trauma room. Very bright lights, medical staff, and machines were everywhere. Bill met us there, and before I could talk to him and explain what had just happened, I felt like I needed to talk to Dr. Kendra. I made a promise to Brent, and I did not want to break it. Since Bill was with Brent, I felt like it was a good time for me to talk to her out in the hall. I told her that I thought I knew what was happening and that I wanted her to know what I had promised Brent. She listened quietly, and together we agreed on a treatment plan. I asked her to talk to Bill and to discuss the treatment plan we came up with once I was back in the room. She explained the situation to Bill, and again Bill, Brent, and I were on the same page. We spent the next two hours quietly praying, standing, and waiting. I was hopeful that we still had some time left. I knew it wouldn't be much, but I figured that we had at least a few days. We were anxiously waiting to get Brent settled in his room. Once there we were going to call home and let him talk to his siblings. The transport team came just as Brent said his last words: "I love you too!" What happened next was *ugly*. It's something no parent should ever have to witness. With Bill at my side and Jesus breathing for me, I know Brent was welcomed home.

I never imagined myself wanting to leave my child's lifeless body. I imagined myself *never* being able to let go. Brent was no longer there, and he no longer needed me. My heart was aching for the others, and I desperately wanted to go home and be with them. Planning a funeral or anything else was not important to me. Brent passed away at 1:30 a.m. I called a few family and friends from the hospital. My mom wanted to know if they should come. I said no, and after taking care of several details, Bill and I left the hospital and arrived back home around 5:00 a.m. Bill and I were both exhausted and numb. The extreme silence was deafening. I immediately found myself sobbing in Brent's bed. *How* could he be gone? It just didn't seem real. We both decided to try to sleep, but we didn't sleep for long. Nicholas, Justin, Kevin, and Corrina were staying at my parent's house. I needed to see them, but I wasn't sure what to say, or how to tell them. Later that morning when we stopped over to my mom's house, the kids were being typical: happy, full of energy, and excited that we were there.

"But where is Brent?" they all asked.

They were hoping to see him, and feeling so empty, I could barely get the words out: "Brent died last night."

Sorry, gotta go, time to make funeral arrangements. If I could rewind time, I would have just sat there and cried my eyes out with Nicholas, Justin, Kevin, and Corrina. I wanted to let everything else stop and help them through their pain. Instead we were off to pick out flowers, a burial plot at the cemetery, and a casket. Then we had to plan the service and somehow try to put together memory boards. I just kept thinking just one more thing: *When this is over … then …*

I am so thankful for the people who did step up to help. Our neighbors brought over a ham with all the fixings. My mom had planned several funerals and knew just what to do. Like clockwork, we went from the florist to the cemetery to the funeral home. Each stop became more and more difficult for me. I wanted balloons at Brent's funeral. I hated and still hate the typical funeral arrangements. They scream death. I was not in denial, but in my heart I did *not* and still do not consider him dead, just gone. I know that he is alive and healthy in heaven. I believe heaven is for real and one day we will be together again. At one time during Brent's illness, I had asked Brent if he wanted anything special at his service. He politely told me that he didn't care, and that whatever we chose to do would be fine with him. The funeral home was the last place we needed to go, and when we got there, I wanted to leave. We were greeted by the owner, and he was very respectful. Decisions, decisions, decisions, needed to be made, and I was not feeling very decisive. We discussed times, dates, and services, and then the ultimate *yuck*—choosing a casket. Yeah, okay, leave me out of this decision. We walked into the casket room, and I lost it. I immediately went back to the office and just sat there and cried. Bill, my mom, and Mark came back into the room. Mark opened a brochure and showed us a picture of a casket that was designed specifically so people could sign it. It was made from a light shade of wood, and it came with a rainbow set of permanent markers. Yes, that was the one. I'd never seen anything like it, and to me it seemed perfect. Balloons and a casket you could sign. I know my mom thought that I was losing it, but she went along with it. Bill was uncomfortable too, not just with the decisions I was making but with the planning as well.

Now came time to plan the service. Donna and Pastor Sam came over to our house. We'd been attending a small local church for almost two years when Brent passed away, and I'd never met Donna until that day. She was the women's ministry leader and also the most compassionate, comforting, and encouraging person I'd ever met. Secretly I thought she was an angel sent by the Lord Himself. She just listened as we sobbed and cried. Donna wanted to know about Brent and spent time looking through pictures with us.

Organization is probably not one of my strongest points. I'd never put together baby books for the kids, but I did manage to separate their pictures for a slide show that I had professionally made when we celebrated Brent's tenth birthday. It was a huge celebration. We celebrated Brent's life and the lives of the rest of our kids as well. Nick, Justin, Kevin, and Corrina were dedicated that same day. We had over one hundred guests celebrating with us. The pictures had been put away in a "safe" place, and now that I needed them, I was in no frame of mind to find them. I'm still really good at putting things in a safe place and then forgetting where I put them. I called my friend Teri to come over and put together the memory boards while Donna, Bill, and I selected pictures from the extra bins I found. Thankfully my sister Pam loved taking photos because most of the ones we used to celebrate Brent's life were the photos she had taken and passed along to me. The wake and funeral were exhausting. I don't really remember much. I did feel the strength and courage that came from the Lord. This letter was the most encouraging thing that day. I felt terrible that Brent wasn't able to get baptized, yet amazed at how God assured all of us.

Thursday, July 18, 2002

Dear Kathy,

I just wanted you to know that I was praying for Brent last night and this morning. He was very heavy on my mind. This morning, I was still praying for him in the shower and I asked the Lord if he could be okay for his baptism. I then started speaking these words which I don't believe were my own as the water was coming down: "I baptize you (Brent) in the name of the Father, Son and Holy Spirit." I knew then and there that Brent had gone to be with His Heavenly Father and that he was truly "baptized" in God's sight.

In Christ's Service,

Sue

Sue

Not only were the wake and funeral exhausting, but I was also taken aback by how insensitive some of the people were who came to pay their respects. Obviously they didn't understand Brent's medical condition and were not pleased with our decision to let Brent make the most of the time he had left. One person in particular really got under my skin.

When it was time for her to say her condolences, she simply said, "Well, looks like you got what you wanted."

I seriously can't think of any mother who would want to be attending a funeral for their child. It's taken me some time to realize that God doesn't control people and that people say *stupid* things. I've also learned that attending someone's funeral is mostly a way to show support to the friends and family who are grieving. If I may add a little advice, it's that if you can't be respectful—don't attend.

9

I Am: Forever Changed

"Neither this man nor his parents sinned," said Jesus, "but this happened so that the works of God might be displayed in him."

—John 9:3 NIV

Portrait of Brent with his head tilted slightly, smiling big

I AM by Brent Vaughan

Smart
An Egypt fanatic
A musician
Good at memorizing
Obedient
Helpful
A Christian
Thankful
Honest

⌣

I love the way Brent described himself in this simple poem that he wrote. His life was such a gift to everyone who knew him. Yes, I am still sad that he's not here, but the memories I have give me strength and peace to go on. Brent was really smart—maybe too smart. I remember when he was being tested to be placed in the gifted program. He came home from school and told me that he didn't do well on the test intentionally because he realized that being in the gifted program would require more work. To Brent, school was all about socializing. He was obedient, helpful, and thankful beyond any parent's dreams. My greatest wish has since changed after Brent's death. He was a Christian, and it showed. His courage, strength, and selfless attitude still amaze me. Now my greatest wish has turned into a lifelong prayer. I consistently pray for all my children to know the Lord, to love Him, and to serve Him. Brent lost his health, but through his journey, his faith increased. Brent lost his physical strength, but he developed indescribable courage through the power of the Holy Spirit living in him. Brent surrendered his future and gained eternity in heaven through his faith in Christ. I am confident of that.

10

My Favorite Things: What I Miss Most

And if I go and prepare a place for you, I will come back and take you to be with me that you also may be where I am.

—John 14:3 NIV

Brent on a tire swing laughing

My Favorite Things:

My favorite TV show is, *Whose Line is it Anyway?*
My favorite radio station is 106.7 F.M. "The Fish."
My favorite magazine is *Breakaway.*
My favorite newspaper (even though I don't really read any) would have to be the *Daily Herald.*
My favorite hobbies are playing video games, riding my bike, and wrestling with my brothers.
My favorite pet was an algae-eating fish we named Licky.
My favorite daydream was about me finding an ancient Egyptian tomb that was never opened and becoming rich and famous.

Three of my favorite books are *My Life as a Burrito with Extra Hot Sauce,* *My Life as Reindeer Road Kill,* and *My Life as Dinosaur Dental Floss.* My three favorite movies are *The Mummy, The Mummy Returns,* and *The Prince of Egypt.* I've been to Florida, Minnesota, Indiana, Michigan, Tennessee, Georgia, Alabama, and Kentucky. A major experience I had was my heart transplant.

———

As strange as it may sound, the thing I miss the most about Brent are his hands. His hands were the very first thing I noticed when he was born. His hands have created many silly treasures that we still have displayed around the house. It was incredible to watch him draw. He'd grab a pencil or whatever happened to be near and went for it. He didn't sketch, erase, or scribble … he simply directed the lines to form the most interesting pieces. His drawings were filled with emotion and always made me smile. His hands grew large, just like his dad. We'd laugh as he compared his to mine. My absolute favorite thing about his hands was when I got to hold them. As soon as he was old enough to travel in the front seat of the car, we'd secretly hold hands. We didn't do this all the time, just the days we were heading to the hospital or the doctor's office. His hands were strong, gentle, caring, thankful, and giving, just like his heart.

I also miss Brent's smile. I used to tell him that when he smiled his whole face smiled. His eyes, nose, and mouth all cooperated to create a lasting impression. He always found humor in any situation, so I remember that his face was consistently smiling. It's funny, but he asked me if he was going to have glasses in heaven. I told him that he probably wouldn't need them since his body was going to be made brand new! He insisted that he would have glasses because he liked the way he looked when he was wearing them. Once he said that I realized that the only time Brent wasn't wearing his glasses was when he was sleeping.

I also miss the countless people who are no longer a part of my everyday life. For example, I miss Sherrie. Sherrie was the transplant coordinator at the hospital in Chicago. She was our lifeline. Sherrie was sweet—her voice, her manners, her face. She was someone you would say was just as beautiful on the outside as she was on the inside. It's hard for me to imagine Sherrie ever having a life away from her work. She was always available. I really miss her! Her reassuring counsel and expert advice helped us through many difficult nights. An occasional Christmas card with a personal note still brings joy!

Ann became more like a sister than a friend. We met downtown. Our boys shared the same diagnosis at birth, and together we shared our journeys. We laughed, cried, and cooked most of our dinners together while talking on the phone. Ann and I parted ways for a time. Brent's illness frightened her, and watching her son, Bill, thrive was painful for me. We reunited several years later, just weeks before her son was diagnosed with something similar to Brent. Bill continues on his journey after his second transplant. I keep in touch with Ann, but it's just not the same. We used to share our fears, dreams, and lab results. Now we share what God is teaching us through the good times and bad.

I miss the craziness of having five energetic children laughing at the dinner table, scrambling to get out of the minivan, and helping with the endless piles of laundry. I miss the excitement of Halloween costumes, shopping for Christmas presents, and birthday party celebrations. In spite of all I miss, I know that one day we will all be together, celebrating in an endless eternity with God Almighty. I can't think of anything better than that. I am thankful for the hope I have in Christ.

So you're probably wondering why I decided to title this book *Apples from Heaven*. Well, let me tell you that these are no ordinary apples. On March 26, 1990, Brent received a crab apple tree for his first birthday from his grandma and papa. Over the years we cared for it, pruned it, and enjoyed its springtime blossoms. The tree grew larger and larger, delighting our backyard. Its small crab apples fell to the ground and sometimes sprouted into little saplings.

The very first spring after Brent died, the tree bloomed brightly pink as it had in the past. As the days passed, the tiny crab apples grew larger and larger. People began to notice, and so did we. Ever since that first year without Brent, we've had apples. *Many apples!* I always look forward to spring as I know we will have apples again.

Kathy holding apples from Brent's tree